Bear Island

Indigenous Americas

Robert Warrior and Jace Weaver, Series Editors

Daniel Heath Justice, *Our Fire Survives the Storm: A Cherokee Literary History*

Thomas King, *The Truth About Stories: A Native Narrative*

Gerald Vizenor, *Bear Island: The War at Sugar Point*

Robert Warrior, *The People and the Word: Reading Native Nonfiction*

Robert A. Williams, Jr., *Like a Loaded Weapon: The Rehnquist Court, Indian Rights, and the Legal History of Racism in America*

Bear Island

THE WAR AT SUGAR POINT

Gerald Vizenor

FOREWORD BY JACE WEAVER

Indigenous Americas

UNIVERSITY OF MINNESOTA PRESS

MINNEAPOLIS

LONDON

The University of Minnesota Press gratefully acknowledges
assistance provided for the publication of this book by the John K.
and Elsie Lampert Fesler Fund.

Published by the University of Minnesota Press
111 Third Avenue South, Suite 290
Minneapolis, MN 55401-2520
http://www.upress.umn.edu

Library of Congress Cataloging-in-Publication Data

Vizenor, Gerald Robert, 1934–
    Bear Island : the war at Sugar Point / Gerald Vizenor ;
    foreword by Jace Weaver.
       p. cm. — (Indigenous Americas)
    ISBN 0-8166-4699-6 (acid-free paper)
    1. United States. Army. Infantry Regiment, 3rd—Poetry. 2. Ojibwa
Indians—Poetry.   I. Title. II. Series.
    PS3572.I9B43 2006
    811'.54—dc22

                                      2005030560

Printed in the United States of America on acid-free paper

The University of Minnesota is an equal-opportunity educator and
employer.

12 11 10 09 08 07 06   10 9 8 7 6 5 4 3 2 1

Liberty is poorly served by men whose good intent is quelled from one failure or two failures or any number of failures, or from the casual indifference or ingratitude of the people, or from the sharp show of the tushes of power, or the bringing to bear soldiers and cannon or any penal statutes. Liberty relies upon itself, invites no one, promises nothing, sits in calmness and light, is positive and composed, and knows no discouragement.
—WALT WHITMAN, *Leaves of Grass*

An intimate geographical knowledge of the country is also required by a successful war leader, and such a man piques himself not only upon knowing every prominent stream, hill, valley, wood, or rock, but the peculiar productions, mineral and vegetable, of the scene of operations.
—WILLIAM WARREN, *History of the Ojibway Nation*

Contents

Foreword

JACE WEAVER

The Third United States Infantry, established in 1784 as the First American Regiment, was the storied veteran of many imperial campaigns. Created by act of Congress, it formed the nucleus of the regular United States Army. William Henry Harrison commanded it on the Canadian border during the War of 1812, after which it was rechristened as the Third Infantry. In 1840, it was sent to Florida to fight the Second Seminole War. Under Winfield Scott, it stormed the ramparts of Chapultepec. As a result of its hard-charging service in the Mexican War, it was given the rare distinction of being permitted to pass in review with bayonets fixed. During the Spanish-American War, it fought its way from San Juan Hill to Santiago before returning home to the safety of Fort Snelling in Minnesota.

For thirty-five years following the end of the American Civil War, the Third Infantry and units like it secured the United States' Manifest Destiny, ensuring the expansion of the "area of freedom" (in Andrew Jackson's phrase) through the dispossession of the continent's indigenes, while fear gripped a nation. "Waiting for the word from the West" was a reluctant pastime of a worried populace. All that was believed to have been rendered unnecessary, however, with the dying echo of Hotchkiss guns over the killing fields of the Wounded Knee. Now, in 1898, eight years after the United States' proclamation of "Mission Accomplished" in the Indian

Wars, three years after Frederick Jackson Turner calmed jangled nerves when, at a celebration of the four hundredth anniversary of Columbus's "discovery," he declared the end of the Frontier, newspapers stunned previously complacent readers with headlines like "Troops Battle Savages." Rumors spread of a massacre akin to Custer's. Home less than a month from Cuba, the Third Infantry had been ordered out of its barracks to fight Indians one more time.

The incident that Gerald Vizenor relates so brilliantly in this, his first epic poem (he plans more), really happened. Were it not for the fact that six recruits died for no good reason—as is usually the case in imperial adventures—it would bear all the hallmarks of satire, a kind of late-nineteenth-century *Mouse That Roared*.

Bugonaygeshig, Hole in the Day, a chief of the Pillager Band of Anishinaabe, demeaningly called "Old Bug" by white colonial masters, was arrested for suspected involvement in liquor trafficking and brought to Duluth, Minnesota, for trial. When the charges were dismissed for lack of evidence, he was released and left to make his way a hundred miles back to his Leech Lake reservation by his own devices. Walking the distance and arriving home sick and weak, he swore never again to collaborate with the colonizer's judicial system.

In late September 1898, when Bugonaygeshig came in to the Onigum Agency at Leech Lake to pick up his annuity payment, he was arrested for refusing to answer a summons to testify in federal court in connection with another whiskey-selling case. He shouted out for help, and some twenty-two Natives, including at least three women, answered his call, spiriting him away from the authorities. Marshal Robert Morrison and Arthur Tinker, the inspector of agencies, panic-stricken and embarrassed by their own incompetence, reported that a "vicious mob" of two hundred Anishinaabe warriors had attacked and overpowered them. They requested military assistance.

On September 30, a raw second lieutenant of the Third Infantry arrived with twenty-two men. For three days they kept vigil while

Morrison and Tinker negotiated futilely with the Anishinaabe for the surrender of Hole in the Day. Reinforcements were requested, and seventy-seven additional soldiers, under the command of a General Bacon and brevet Major Melville Wilkinson came, arriving on October 4.

The following day, the army contingent, accompanied by newspaper reporters, set out by barge and steamship for Bear Island, where Hole in the Day was reportedly holed up. Finding the place deserted, the force moved on to Sugar Point, site of Hole in the Day's homestead. Once again they saw no one. Unaware that they were surrounded and being watched, they prepared to make camp. As the troops were stacking their arms, one rifle fell over and discharged. Thinking they had been discovered, the Indians opened fire. The soldiers fired back at shadows and spent an anxious night shivering in the cold, scared and under constant threat.

Two days later, Bacon's forwarded dispatch arrived at the War Department in Washington: "Commenced fighting at 11:30 yesterday. Indians seem to have best position. Not moving. Maj. Wilkinson, five soldiers and two Indian police killed; awaiting reinforcements." The word had once again, and very unexpectedly, arrived from the West. The *Potsdam–St. Lawrence Herald* in New York carried a front-page headline: "An Indian Uprising." Subheads read "Fighting with United States Troops in Minnesota—A Hot Fight" and "Indians in Bad Mood." "The Indian troubles in Minnesota have suddenly assumed a very serious aspect," the article began. "A detachment of soldiers under command of General Bacon was attacked by a strong body of Indians on Bear Island, Leech Lake, about thirty miles from Walker, Minn. and a hot fight ensued, which lasted nearly all day. It is feared General Bacon's command has been massacred." The "strong body" of Indian warriors was actually only nineteen men, most of whom melted away during the night. Hole in the Day was never reliably placed at the scene.

Even before the word arrived from the West, the War at Sugar Point was over. On the evening of October 6, 214 Minnesota militia, armed with a Gatling gun, arrived in Walker by train. The following day, as they headed for Bear Island, they were met by the previously besieged Third Infantry, coming from the other direction. The Pillager warriors had simply let them withdraw.

The underlying causes of the "war" were all too familiar, sounding sadly similar to those that provoked Little Crow's War in the same region a generation earlier in 1862. In 1933, Colonel Henry Wurdemann, an adopted Anishinaabe who had served as secretary to United States Senator Joseph Quarles during the congressional investigation of the incident, published an account of the skirmish and the subsequent investigation: Treaty payments, of which little actually reached the hands of the Native recipients. Uncaring Indian agents. Capricious treatment of Indians. It was reported that there were desecrations of Indian graves. And Indians were being cheated out of revenues from timbering on their lands. In the aftermath of the engagement—as always happened—changes were promised.

Following the uprising, the American public once more cocooned itself in a blanket of denial, ignoring its culpability for what had occurred. The incident was erased from conscious memory. The Indian Wars still ended on the frozen ground of Dakota Territory. Today, the Leech Lake Tourism Bureau, discussing Hole in the Day's resistance, states, "That last vestige of the old century was followed by a new century of building . . . lodges, hotels, resorts, campgrounds, steamboats, sternwheelers, dance pavilion and floating resort, excursion boats (one of which was 135 feet long), roads, canals, dams, libraries, schools, churches . . . right up to today's shops, stores, restaurants, theaters, casinos, marinas, national forest, state parks, and so much more." The Cliffs Notes of theft and dispossession.

By 1898, though they themselves did not know it, Native Americans were already forgotten. The American nation had turned its attention to a wider Manifest Destiny to be fulfilled in the Caribbean and the Pacific, in places like Cuba, Puerto Rico, the Philippine Islands, and Hawaii. With the Spanish-American War, the United States defeated a European colonizer and willed itself into a world power, a status ratified by World War I. The "Empire of Liberty" had reached its limits in North America, and new territories had to be found. No longer content to stay at home and merely be an example to the world, the Puritans' "shining city on a hill," the nation now felt compelled to impose its model upon others. Indians had been pacified and were, quite simply, irrelevant.

Hole in the Day scoured the ground, collecting cartridge casings. He strung these into a necklace, which he wore with pride. He was photographed wearing the strand, a rifle slung at the ready, cradled in his left arm. Before he died in 1918, he saw the U.S. Forest Service take over management of all national forest lands and the creation of a huge national forest encompassing ceded Anishinaabe territory. He saw the peaceful and profitable sale of fish and maple syrup to whites. And he witnessed Anishinaabes and whites fighting side by side in the United States Army during World War I. Still, he prized his war trophy necklace. When he passed away, he was one of the most respected individuals in the area.

The Third Infantry went on to other imperial conflicts. From 1899 to 1902, it battled *insurrectos* in the Philippines. And a century later, its namesake, the Third Infantry Division (or 3rd I.D., in macho Defense Department shorthand), spearheaded the thrust into Iraq. When the Pentagon was attacked on September 11, 2001, the "Old Guard" Third Infantry, headquartered at Fort Myers, Virginia, was one of the first units on the scene.

The Indian Wars are long forgotten in the popular memory. The flurry of panic in October 1898 mimics the color-coded hysteria of terrorism since 9/11. Once more a nervous citizenry waits for the next shoe to drop. It no longer waits for the word from the West. Instead, it awaits that word from the Middle East, or Afghanistan, or Indonesia, or even from here at home. It waits and is afraid, just as afraid as that same citizenry was during westward expansion. After "regime change" and an American-mandated election in Iraq, the Empire of Liberty is once more on the march.

Bear Island

Introduction

The War at Sugar Point

The Anishinaabe observed the *miigis,* the *midewiwin* spiritual shell, or cowrie, as a source of visionary presence in the northern woodland lakes. The Grand Medicine Society, *midewiwin,* is an association of Native healers and shamans. The *miigis* arose from the eastern sea and moved westward with the natural course of the sun. The Anishinaabe origin stories count the *miigis* for the last time in *gichigami,* the great sea, or Lake Superior.

The Anishinaabe envisioned their associations with the earth by natural reason, by tricky stories, and by *odoodemi,* to have a totem, an imagic sense of presence in the time and seasons of the woodland lakes.

The Anishinaabe trickster, *naanabozho,* is forever imagined by native storiers. The trickster, crafty or humane, is an uncertain, existential shaman of creation, a healer by stories, and a comic transformation in mythic time—comic in the sense that the imagic presence of a trickster is a figurative trace of survivance, not a tragic revision of dominance or misadventure in the racial sentiments of monotheistic civilization.

The Anishinaabe created five traditional totems, the natural images of families and ancestry. The original five totems are the *ajijaak* (the sandhill crane), *makwa* (the bear), *maanameg* (the catfish), *waabizheshi* (the marten), and *maang* (the loon). William Warren, the nineteenth-century Anishinaabe historian, wrote in *History of the Ojibway Nation* that the other totems, or "different badges," are "only subdivisions of the five great original totems." Natives of the *ajijaak* (the crane totem) are orators and leaders. The *makwa* (bear totem) are bold and brave warriors. The three other totems are figures of a communal presence in the natural world.

Sugar Point is a trace of creation and the modern site of a war enacted by the United States Army in 1898. The Anishinaabe had resisted the arrogant and capricious federal marshals and then routed, by imagination, natural reason, stealth, and strategy, the imperious officers and immigrant soldiers from the Leech Lake Reservation. That defeat is seldom mentioned in military histories.

Sugar Point, or Battle Point, is near Bear Island, south of Portage Bay and Federal Dam in the eastern section of Leech Lake. The Mississippi River, or *gichiziibi,* the great river, runs through the Leech Lake Reservation in north central Minnesota. The reservation was established by federal treaty in 1855. Lake Winnibigoshish, Leech Lake, Cass Lake, Squaw Lake, and many other lakes are within the original treaty boundaries of the reservation. Onigum, a Native community, is located on the reservation between Walker Bay and Agency Bay.

The Pillagers of Leech Lake are one of the original five clans of the Anishinaabe. The totemic families are *makwa* (bear) and *maanameg* (catfish), and the warriors are admired for their courage, independent spirit, and resistance to federal agents and policy. The Pillagers and Dakota once competed for the buffalo hunting grounds on the peneplain at the western verge of the woodland, and their Native tact and diplomacy wavered for centuries between war and peace.

Alexander Henry, the determined eighteenth-century fur trader, named the spirited Natives of Leech Lake and Bear Island the Pilleurs. Edward Neill observed in *History of the Ojibways* that on August 5, 1775, "at Rat Portage, some of the Ojibways asked for rum, but Henry refused, because they were the band of the

Pilleurs." The French word *pilleur* means "pillager." That prejudi-cial designation was the first historical notice of the Native warriors named the Pillagers.

Chief Flat Mouth, one of the great leaders of the Pillagers, was mentioned in the journals of Zebulon Pike, a narrative on the source of the Mississippi River in 1805. William Warren noted that Flat Mouth first met Pike at the Northwest Fur Company post at Leech Lake and traded his British standard and peace medal for the colors of the United States of America. Flat Mouth "ceased to be an Englishman and became a Long Knife," or an American.

Great Britain had sought the support and loyalty of Flat Mouth and the Pillagers against the Americans in the War of 1812. War-ren wrote that crown agents were "sent by the British government to the principal villages of the Ojibways, to invite them to join their arms against the Americans." The British agents presented wam-pum belts as an obligatory gratuity. Flat Mouth promptly returned the bounty and told the agent, "When I go war against my ene-mies, I do not call on the whites to join my warriors. The white people have quarreled among themselves, and I do not wish to meddle in their quarrels, nor do I intend ever, even to be guilty of breaking the window glass of a white man's dwelling."

Keeshkemun, or Sharpened Stone, the distinguished Native leader at Lac du Flambeau, ingeniously shunned a similar entreaty by crown agents of Great Britain. The Anishinaabe orator countered the political summons with avian metaphors of Native resistance.

Keeshkemun was asked by the agent to identify himself and explain his position, reported Warren. "If you wish to know me, you must seek me in the clouds. I am a bird who rises from the earth, and flies far up, into the skies, out of human sight; but though not visible to the eye, my voice is heard from afar, and resounds over the earth!" Keeshkemun was a member of the crane totem. "You have never sought me, or you should have found and known me. Others have sought and found me. The old French sought and found me. He placed his heart within my breast," said Keeshkemun.

"He told me that if troubles assailed me, to arise in the skies and cry to him, and he would hear my voice. He told me that his fire would last forever, to warm me and my children." Englishman, "you have put out the fire of my French father. I became cold and needy, and you sought me not. Others have sought me. Yes, the Long Knife has found me. He has placed his heart on my breast."

The Pillagers were secure at the end of the territorial wars between Great Britain and the United States, but six years later that cultural assurance became chancy. Black Dog and sixteen warriors "marched westward and proceeded further into the country of their enemies," the Dakota, wrote Warren. The Pillager warriors crossed the prairie and "discovered a large encampment of Dakotas." Black Dog and his warriors were outnumbered and soon surrounded by buffalo hunters on horseback.

The Pillagers "each dug a hole in the ground" in a "clump of poplar trees" on the prairie. The Dakota were painted for war and "suffered a severe loss from the unerring aim of their desperate enemies, who threw not a single shot away," observed Warren. The Pillager "supply of ammunition gave out, and the Dakotas discovering it by the slackening of their fire, and by one of their number being wounded with a stone which an Ojibway had substituted in his gun for a bullet, a simultaneous rush was made on them, and after a short hand to hand struggle, the sixteen Pillager warriors, with but one exception, were killed." Bugaunak "returned safely to his people, but he never would give but the most supernatural account of his manner of escape—tales that were not believed by his own people," wrote Warren. Later, however, the "Dakotas acknowledged that they lost thirty-three of their warriors in this desperate engagement." The word *bugaunak* is transcribed as *pagwana* in *A Dictionary of the Otchipwe Language* by Bishop Baraga, and *bagwana* in *A Concise Dictionary of Minnesota Ojibwe* by John D. Nichols and Earl Nyholm. The words *pagwana* and *bagwana* are translated as "at random," "by chance," "anyhow," and "by heart." *Bagwana* is translated as "by my heart" in this narrative.

Bugonaygeshig, or *bagone giizhig,* "hole in the day," an eminent and historic name in translation, was a Native *midewiwin* healer. The Pillager warrior was born on Bear Island in 1836. He lived in a cabin at Sugar Point. Bugonaygeshig was the third Native to bear that notable name.

Old Bug, a pejorative nickname concocted by federal agents, was arrested with another Native in September 1898 at the Onigum Agency on the Leech Lake Reservation. They had refused to testify in federal court about the felonious sale of alcoholic beverages on the reservation. Robert Morrison, the federal deputy marshal, and Colonel Arthur Tinker, the inspector of agencies, led the "reluctant witnesses to the boat that would take them on the first leg of their journey to Duluth," wrote Roger Pinckney in "Old Bug's Necklace."

The Northern Minnesota Publishing Company reported in "Last Indian War in the United States, October 1898" that the old "chief was taken by the marshal and spirited down to the lake front." Bugonaygeshig called out, "Where are my young men?" Some "twenty of his braves swooped down and released him. They all fled to the security of the forest, and the marshal returned empty handed, and the bright, white light of the white man's peace was dulling in the shadows." Marshal Morrison overstated the scene and requested immediate military assistance. "Federal authorities issued warrants for the arrest of the two fugitives and for twenty of those who had abetted their escape," wrote Pinckney. The Third Infantry, a company of seventy-seven enlisted men and two officers, arrived a few days later. The soldiers boarded two steamers that cold morning, October 5, 1898, and three hours later over rough waves arrived at Sugar Point.

Pinckney reported that nineteen armed Natives waited at the tree line. The soldiers expeditiously occupied the cabin and vegetable garden of Hole in the Day at Sugar Point. The war started by chance that morning when a recruit stacked his rifle but forgot to engage the safety. "Another man stumbled against the rifles, the stack collapsed, and the unsecured weapon sent a bullet skipping across the ground toward where the Ojibwe lay hiding. Stories from the Indian side tell of several soldiers firing at a canoe-load of women who were on their way to beg release of the captives on the steamer."

Major Melville Cary Wilkinson, "in the tradition of Civil War officers, boldly walked among his men, in clear view of the enemy, directing fire and offering encouragement. It was not a good idea," observed Pinckney. "First he lost the skin on an elbow, then a bullet punctured a hole through his thigh. He was hauled behind the cabin to have his wounds dressed. Shortly thereafter, Wilkinson hobbled back into the line of fire and took a bullet in the belly. 'Give 'em hell,' were his last words to General Bacon."

One Native warrior is "said to have run from cover, climbed atop a rail fence, and yelled, 'They can't hit anything!' He stood there laughing as bullets whistled around him, then jumped back into the brush."

Nathan Dally reported in the *Cass County Pioneer* that the last soldier was killed while "digging some potatoes as it was getting light the next morning. He was fired at by Bug's fifteen year old son who was prowling around his father's home in the uncertain light, but his first shot missed and the soldier ran back into the house, but he said, 'I am going to get those potatoes anyway,' and went back. The boy's next shot finished him."

The Third Infantry was surrounded and shivered overnight without provisions. The Pillagers, only nineteen warriors, outmaneuvered more than seventy immigrant soldiers and won the war in a single day. Major Wilkinson and five soldiers were dead and eleven were wounded in the garden at Sugar Point. There were no reports of Native casualties.

"I must confess," wrote George Wicker, "that I dreaded to fire my gun at the unfortunate red man. I felt that he was but fighting for the land, country, and the rights that were his, fighting, it is true, in his own peculiar and treacherous way. Later on I learned that these sentiments were shared by many of those who with me at that time wore the blue." Wicker was a private in the Third

Infantry. He published his story, "In the Battle with the Chippe-was," in *Home Journal,* a year after the war at Sugar Point.

"There were and are men in high places who have oppressed, defrauded, robbed, insulted, maltreated the Indian, the rightful owner of this country, until the poor savage could no longer endure his wrongs," declared Wicker. "He, too, loves his forests, lakes, streams, his native soil."

Five newspaper reporters covered the war at Sugar Point. Their stories were telegraphed overnight to newspapers around the country. Kenneth Beaton reported for the *Minneapolis Tribune.* A. F. Morton reported for the *Saint Paul Globe.*

William Hascal Brill wrote for the Associated Press and the *Daily Pioneer Press* on October 7, 1898, that the "battle of Leech Lake is over. The bodies of six soldiers for whom taps has been sounded for the last time and eleven severely wounded men, lying in the old warehouse near the dock in Walker, tell the story of its severity as far as the boys in blue are concerned." The Third Infantry "took part in both the battle of El Caney and that of San Juan and lost three men killed. In the battle of Leech Lake a part of one company was engaged and six men gave up their lives. And yet the battles before Santiago de Cuba were called fierce once and the battle of Leech Lake was a skirmish and history will probably overlook it," wrote Brill.

"And the pity of it all is that it seems so useless. For what object, what principle did Major Wilkinson die and his men lose their lives from Indian bullets? Simply that a few Indians did not wish to go to Duluth to testify against a man that sold them whiskey. Still the authority of the government must be preserved and brave men must give up their lives that a whiskey seller may be given sixty days in jail. The soldiers cared and knew nothing about this trouble, but they gave their lives in support of their oaths and allegiance."

Bemidji, Cass Lake, and many other nearby towns prepared for war. Citizens were worried that the army could not defend their families and property. Louis Raddis reported in "The Last Indian

Uprising in the United States," first published by the Minnesota Historical Society, that there was panic in Bemidji. "The women were collected in the court house and two hundred armed citizens kept watch and ward. The arrival of detachments of troops in the villages soon quieted the alarm and caused the excitement to subside."

William Jones, United States Commissioner of Indian Affairs, traveled from Washington to Walker, Minnesota. He arrived on October 10, 1898, and met with the Pillagers at Bear Island. Louis Raddis pointed out that the Native leaders acceded to the warrants issued by federal marshals and arrested the Native warriors who had defended Hole in the Day a few weeks earlier at Onigum Agency.

"When their cases came before Judge Lochren on October 21, 1898, all were found guilty and were given sentences varying from sixty days imprisonment and a fine of twenty-five dollars to ten months and one hundred dollars," wrote Raddis. "On December 13, the Indian office recommended that the term of imprisonment be commuted to two months and that the fines be remitted, and finally on June 3, 1899, the pardons were granted."

The Pillagers bravely resisted the federal policies that spurned their Native rights and eroded their sacred land. Roger Pinckney pointed out that relations with Natives had deteriorated when "Minneapolis flour millers persuaded Congress to regulate the flow of the Mississippi by building a series of dams on lakes at the headwaters of the river." The rising water flooded Native communities, and with no notice "drowned beds of wild rice, and washed the bones of Indian dead upon the shore." The Pillagers "bitterly complained that they were being defrauded by white speculators who were illegally harvesting timber from their lands."

Pillager warriors, outnumbered more than three to one, routed the soldiers of the Third Infantry in a single day, October 5, 1898. The army casualties were six dead and eleven wounded, a certain defeat seldom mentioned in military histories.

Overture

Manidoo Creations

the anishinaabe
natives of the miigis
fugitive rivers
canoe birch
white pine
face the clouds
and cedar boughs

worthy hunters
cut the barren
masks of hunger
boreal shadows
eternal spirits
on the ancient stone

crafty trickster
naanabozho
created natives
bears and cranes
muskrats
beaver moves
by sorrow and tease
arouses stories
lonesome
uncertain scenes
blue and watery

october storms
turn and rush
across leech lake
great waves
break on shore
at bear island
native colors heave
elusive otters
trace the bay
ravens bounce
on the main
and wolves await
the sacred rise
of sandhill cranes
over the birch
feathers and praise
at sunrise

manidoo creation
blood totems
bear covenants
of native survivance
on the rise
that cold
october morning
at sugar point
natural beats
of chance and liberty

tricky shamans
rout the missions
wily manners
dominance and treason
godly haunts
in fever and fire
prey nearby
at the narrows
windy rush
of muddy water
lust and woe
wounded hearts
unbearable counts
thunder back
overnight
in the black ice

the anishinaabe
trace the seasons
moths and menace
willow catkins
enchanted flight
heartbeats
in the snow
elusive warriors
at the tree line

three centuries
of expatriates
sweaty newcomers

nervy soldiers
soul savages
in heavy uniforms
secede from chance
natural reason
pushed aside
bywords of rank
ironic tribute
clumsy salutes
repeater weapons
godly poses
and liturgy
crash overnight

duty bound
ushers and scalpers
pocket stories
traduce the dance
native stories
scenes of presence
at the mercy
of pious scorn
wicked chantey
confederate cruelty
bounty and hue
of wonted genocide
by first light
outgunned
at sugar point
forever in the book

Bagwana

The Pillagers of Liberty

sugar point
near bear island
south of federal dam
comes to light
creation stories
chance and crusade
memories ashore
native rights
of rivers
ginseng
cedar stands
stolen by grafters
constitutional
greed and guile
stately suits
treaty decadence
over native liberty

anishinaabe warriors
honored forever
among ravens
bright leaves
and chancy shamans
outmaneuvered
the third infantry
that october
trace of costumes

blue shadows
wounded soldiers
shiver alone
at sugar point
wabigamaa
the sandy narrows
bears the name
battle point
on the leech lake
indian reservation

six soldiers dead
bones cracked
muscles torn
bloody wounds
by winchesters
over the turnips
cabbage and potatoes
in a ragged garden
cultivated near shore
by bugonaygeshig
hole in the day
midewiwin healer
and elusive pillager

solitary spirits
marvelous sentiments
of shamans
court and tradition
under the cedar

set by names
ravens and bears
visual memories
traces of bagwana
turned in translation
by my heart
a native warrior
and natural presence
at the tree line

the red sumac
brighten memories
hands and eyes
against the stones
black dog
by my heart
pillager warriors
pictured the scenes
at bear island
in the hazy
morning light
side by side
in tricky moves
kingfishers
cut from a bough
dragonflies
break at sunrise
first shimmer
in the eyes

eternal motion
a native presence

fifteen warriors
by my heart
roused by black dog
loyal dancers
turn to vengeance
track a band
of dakota riders
for the wanton
unforgivable murder
of a pillager child

dakota warriors
braced on horseback
painted for war
circle the avengers
black dog encampment
a shallow burrow
carved by hand
under the cottonwoods
prairie graves
thirty enemy dead
manes unbound
ammunition spent
the plucky pillagers
fired stones
and slowly
turned alone

to songs of death
heard evermore
on the prairie

one pillager
named bagwana
by my heart
survived the war
by slights
rage of light
and vengeance
a raven flight
manidoo nagamon
spirited songs
giant thunderclouds
overturned leaves
a century ago
chased in a storm
by my heart
returned a shaman
silent and alone
to bear island

scent of cedar
silent waxwings
in the sumac
river otters ashore
pillager warriors
dance with the bears
summer colors

on the wing
bright feathers
overnight
faces alight
by the fires
of the anishinaabe

grand medicine
midewiwin
mighty tricks
miigis memories
natural reason
dream songs
creation stories
bear traces
by heat and heart
change the seasons
summer
in the spring
faces on the stone
slight waves
on the silent water
and heal
wounded hearts

midewiwin singers
under cedar boughs
post their colors
spirit cues
and rightly dance

the animals
in natural light
bright and lusty
by my heart
teases feathers
manidoo bounty
abounds in the birch
turns the leaves
ravens circle
great shadows
crease the stones

alexander henry
trader of eminence
out of montreal
contrived the pilleurs
at rat portage
natives accused
nasty names
by marketers
faraway that summer
cursory chase
of a sickly trader
near a creek
so named pillage
nothing more
than a native tease
a tear of calico
unfurled by commerce
returned overnight

but revenge
an evil medicine
cursed the natives
grievous mamakiziwin
spotted faces
byword of smallpox
blisters and death

chief flat mouth
notable name
derived from ashigan
largemouth bass
in translation
menaced the dakota
teased jean nicolet
the explorer
fur trader
boldly protested
provincial
trade prices
set by secrets
and marketers
flat mouth spurned
standby wampum
paltry bounty
empire provisions
trophy agents
pose of liberators
the old chief
wisely reasoned

pillagers of liberty
would never
fight the enemies
of the british crown

chief flat mouth
traded the royal flag
peace medals
and colonial seals
for the new colors
of the long knives
royal covenants
heavenly promises
over every pelt
wild grudges
cause of vengeance
plainly against
the prairie dakota
showy americans
the turn of enemies
territorial vows
country cover
and commerce
never the same
by natural reason
or trace of war
in pillager stories

sharpened stone
keeshkemun

forever honored
by the anishinaabe
crane totem
visionary leader
at lac du flambeau
evaded the british
royal cast
and military summons
a native comeback
by avian metaphors
seek me in the clouds
he gestured
to the crown agents
kingdom officers
i am a bird
out of human sight
and my voice
heard from afar
resounds over the earth

wary ravens
bounced on the dock
at walker bay
twice weary traders
gimoodishkiiwinini
the thieves
strut and gloat
over giant bundles
of ginseng and garlic
native mockery

a breath apart
characters bruised
by devious play
wordy dominance
slight conceits
greedy factors
caught in the dirty
mirrors of civilization

godly triumphalists
almighty traitors
crown the conquest
sneaky treaties
and frontier justice
contrived by grafters
trivial manners
pale indian agents
heave an empire
of stray discoveries
over the dock
an ironic silence
wispy castles
ruins of foam
wash ashore
and justly recede
in the sandy shallows

blue soldiers
barren immigrants
curse totems

native irony
miigis migrations
cowrie stories
faces on the stone
anishinaaabe women
sacred cedar
golden eagle feathers
feral plunders
medicine bundles
midewayaan
cut and bared
on the dock
grave souvenirs
stolen and sold
at great risk

creation stories
stone faces
on the wild rivers
native conversions
birds and bear
tricky unions
hunted and harried
by fatal miners
cruel mountain men
bounty savages
missions of genocide
fear and envy
harrow and hide
deserted for pianos

wainscot and lace
over the natural
native circles
ceremonial feathers
of a mighty
continental liberty

estranged slavers
unrepentant
soldiers mustered
banners raised
mark the righteous
crimes and covenants
against nature
deadly pathogens
sackcloth and smallpox
for natives
patent laudanum
for americans

the colorado militia
wasted forever
the stars and stripes
bloody queues
sinister undertones
frontier treachery
and eternal
cultural separations
at sand creek

continental chance
political liberty
by walt whitman
crucial catchwords
invite no one
promises nothing
but memory
native survivance
timely trickster
stories in the book

generations later
native ghost dancers
hungry children
women on the run
chief big foot
weakened by disease
slaughtered twice
by the colors
revenge for gold
and general custer
cavalry cannons
near the creek
the cruelest
constitutional festival
a prairie genocide
and celebration
of jesus christ
the son of god

born again
that snowy morning
at wounded knee

praise the wind
silver birch
cedar waxwings
and the last
crowns of light
circled by moths
natural moves
and native stories
cocky shamans
rightly tease
frankincense creations
and the deceptions
of treaty men

collars of abraham
deface nature
in the name of god
rage at other creations
stories of chance
convert rivers
unearth the otters
manoomin
native wild rice
buried in reservoirs
city dams

for favored millers
almighty caste
of wealthy names
treacherous barons
of cedar and white pine
copper and gold
crusades and salvation
set by shame
and never court
natural reason
crane migrations
thunderstorms
blueberries in snow
wild cracks of ice
the marvelous poses
of ravens
gaagaagiwag
the godly fear
tricksters and shamans
chance and tease
wild sounds
and that sinister sway
of the city dock
at walker bay

watery creations
moans of monotheism
severe deliverance
burdened by shame

without a crease
of humor or irony
godly tamed
to pray and pity
a sly mastery
over incense and lace
contrite to honor
wolves and beaver
wounded cranes
bearwalkers
at the tree lines
and the sacrifice
of native chance
trickster stories
overnight
at the holy rails
only to celebrate
the lordly separatism
of biblical names

shirty agents
in morning coats
immigrant soldiers
in blue uniforms
decorations of service
bear the cruelty
of american creation
misadventures
wooly and scared

they lost the war
that afternoon
in a vegetable garden
twice cultivated
by hole in the day
a wiry shaman
who lived at sugar point

Hole in the Day

GRAFTERS AND WARRANTS

treacherous waves
break overnight
on leech lake
lanterns out
at the lakeside hotel
on walker bay
boats groan
and beat
an ominous air
against the city dock

natives shiver
at onigum agency
hungry children
bound in blankets
wait outside
for late annuities
demeaned
by treaty ties
federal legacies
overrun by factors
and shady agents

bugonaygeshig
bear island pillager
midewiwin healer
elusive warrior

more than sixty years
the third native
honored by the name
hole in the day
turns his eyes
against the wind
and rides the shadows
with the ravens
that cold morning
at agency bay

colonel tinker
and deputy marshal
robert morrison
bold bounty hunters
served warrants
for the head count
court money
and seized
hole in the day
the pillager
refused to testify
in federal court
against whiskey traders
one more bogus
bootleg trial
mounted in duluth
a hundred miles
from sugar point

hole in the day
roughly shackled
hand to hand
by unscrupulous
federal force
and treaty grounds
shouted out
near the agency
boat dock
where are my young men
twenty warriors
shrouded women
brave children
shy mongrels
and the autumn wind
circled the marshals
bounty posse
ravens bounced
down the rocky shore
a natural dance
and the old warrior
pillager of liberty
escaped in the shadows
at the tree line
praised and protected
by native warriors
nearby at stony point

federal mercenaries
rightly shamed

by native resistance
returned to walker
and broadcast
false stories
disguised as justice
about native fugitives
the mercenaries
overstated the deceptions
of a native menace
by telegram
brashly warned
send the army
civil war generals
brevet patriots
proudly mustered
by doughty dominion
and martial sway
third infantry soldiers
with a gatling gun

bugonaygeshig
was first arrested
months earlier
an elusive suspect
named a wicked
whiskey trader
that april morning
bound to court
with no evidence
but manifest manners

the federal judge
listed at the throne
envious of miters
the scent of polished oak
and gravely declared
mainly the absence
of any testimony
or depositions
by cause of justice
and promptly
dismissed the case

hole in the day
returned to the bears
by natural reason
heard the cause
manners of court
ordered in english
clever comebacks
in anishinaabe
always misconstrued
falsely summoned
then abandoned
by the court
and federal agents
bugonaygeshig
boarded the train
bound for bena
leech lake reservation
an unpaid witness

with no ticket
marooned by race
demeaned by customs
money warrants
rogue factors
and posse grafters
the callous conductor
trenchant about natives
stopped the train
west of duluth
and ousted
the pillager bear
ten miles out
later that day
twice menaced
he was removed
from an empty boxcar

bear island warrior
sixty years old
walked alone
a hundred miles
back to leech lake
and sugar point
overcast with fury
icy spring rain
creases of abuse
visions of resistance
natural reason

wet and weary
moccasins scored
the old pillager
chary of the shoreline
cracked the thin
river verge
and bared
four stately blueberries
brightly frozen
in the clear ice

ravens bounce
and crack
the snow crowns
over the white pines
feathers shimmer
lighten the shrouds
shoulder to wing
praised the summer
in the spring
by dream songs
rosehip bellies
scent of paper birch
near sugar point

hole in the day
never trusted
treaty talk
warrants of commerce

federal mercenaries
over white pine
cedar and willow
river otter
never constitutions
federal dams
documents of credit
court petitions
legal precedent
over bear and beaver
moccasin flowers
natural reason
anishinaabe survivance
and cedar waxwings

indian agents
protect the grafters
over native rights
greedy timber barons
with empty eyes
scorched the pine
slight a name
cut the price
tender fern
wild roses
bare and broken
shadows rage
near the stumps
only stories
stand on treaty land

the gichiziibi
great river
dominion dams
on the mississippi
headwaters
deadly diversions
manoomin
wild rice
and native bones
washed away
sacred otter
menaced by craves
bears unseated
by the surge
at the shoreline
redwinged blackbirds
astray as federal dam
cattails deposed
for power
at the flour mills
downriver in the city

supreme portraits
courts and congress
brushed aside
the constitution
native rights
worthy resistance
steadily dishonored
by wicked grafters

stories bent
against nature
federal marshals
paid by law
for arrest reports
false warrants
captured natives

mighty white pine
native memories
natural motion
wispy spirits
teased the sun
sound of whipsaws
bloody stumps
only shadow stories
over the tender
black fern
a century later
no traces of courage
sentiments of survivance
saved the trees
lathed for banisters
highbrow beams
and city sideboards
exiled forever
in millions of homes
built with timber
clearcut at leech lake

morning coats
never labor
over flour or pine
federal dams
serve the mill masters
flood the seasons
never notice
summer in the spring
never hear
the tease of bears
ceremony of cranes
never see
ravens alight
on the mighty rise
of the white pine

hole in the day
by my heart
native visions
autumn shadows
of liberty
ravens bounce
in the bright leaves
bears advance
with the pillagers
at sugar point
three hours
on a paddle wheel
centuries away

by native rest and sway
from the walker
city dock
vainly named
for a timber baron

Bearwalkers

5 October 1898

brevet major
melville wilkinson
mustachioed
combat commander
third infantry regiment
fort snelling
service in civil
and colonial wars
gallant crusader
plucked the nez perce
from their homeland
by military lies
never imagined
as he marched
down the city dock
at walker bay
saluted the brigadier
general john bacon
department of dakota
unlucky names
and military chance
that cold and miserable
october morning
a slow and miserable
winchester death
by pillager warriors
at sugar point

general bacon
charily boarded
the chief of duluth
a new steamer
on leech lake
owned by the walker
timber company
heaved on the rise
shuddered
against the dock
and slowly
pushed away
in the wake
of black waves

major wilkinson
and seventy seven
wary soldiers
embarked on the flora
a tippy paddle wheel
with two decks
barge in tow
on a brazen mission
to capture
hole in the day
and other pillagers
native fugitives
at sugar point
near bear island

cold hard rain
heavy sleet
turned to snow
icy splinters
driven by wind
portentous waves
pitched the prow
foredeck awash
wooly blue soldiers
wet to the bone
pounded their boots
on the barge deck
to stay warm
sound of worry
untold time
an ominous cadence
lost in the dark
on leech lake
in a wild surge

bearwalkers
spirits of the night
lighted the shore
by my heart
posed at the tree line
a natural crease
erotic shimmer
and naked natives
taunted the soldiers
on the rise

at squaw point
the wild currents
by word and curse
crashed on the narrows
mongrels barked
creatures wheezed
eternal murmur
near goose island
as a pale light
secures the horizon
blaze of maples

lieutenant tenny ross
weighs the distance
port to shore
soldiers hushed
roused by voices
native presence
ablaze in the trees
strain to see
traces of the sunrise
over the waves
breaking on sucker
and traders bay
a tricky solace
for hole in the day
by my heart
and ravens abide
the start of war

the military flotilla
of foolhardy soldiers
newspaper storiers
winced on deck
for three hours
against the waves
fear of reefs
chief of duluth
ran aground
at ottertail point
the flora continued
and anchored
near bear island
clear of the narrows
dangerous landing
by skiff and barge
at sugar point

the pillagers
created a marvelous
natural presence
in red blankets
against the maples
golden birch
soldiers ashore
heavy in the sand
warned the natives
to surrender arms
blue privates
crouch ungainly

near the bright sumac
and ancient stones
on the windy shore
ready to advance
over a spacious garden
turnips and potatoes
cabbage and cucumbers
on the rail fence
against the tree line

cautious platoon
moves on the cabin
built of pine logs
by hole in the day
who was away
among the bears
and ravens
in the maples
and white pine
wary of expatriates
and the wooly stench
of wet uniforms
pushy soldiers
occupy the cabin
midewigaan
medicine lodge
of the old pillager
arrest two dancers
makwa the bear
and george white

who liberated
bugonaygeshig
at onigum agency
and outmaneuvered
colonel tinker
and deputy morrison

no crime at sea
crown dominion
breech of trade
colonial treaty
sneaky constitution
disease or crusade
caused the war
that autumn
under the maples
at sugar point
only the petulance
and deceptions
of federal agents
and military fanatics

makwa the bear
george white
midewiwin dancers
soul healers
removed from the cabin
under heavy guard
and ferried
out to the flora

a paddle wheel prison
anchored clear
of the wild
sandy narrows
five other dancers
native warriors
winchesters in hand
retreated silently
into the maples
and great white pine
unrecognized
by worried soldiers
and federal agents

lieutenant ross
led a combat patrol
three miles north
along the shore
incessant search
for fugitive warriors
and encountered
waaginogaan
birch bark houses
native women
children and elders
circle dancers
a curious soldier
out of time
ate a cooked fish
uncertain irony

of a native giveaway
unbearable silence
at the start of war
empty gaze
hunger soldiers
turned back
by cedar smoke
ravens croak
and native tease
to the midewigaan
and bountiful garden
of hole in the day
at sugar point

nineteen natives
bear island warriors
shrouded at home
in the brush
under the maples
winchesters ready
to scare and menace
untried soldiers
back to the steamer
and recover
the pleasures
of native stories
and medicine dances
by my heart
and hole in the day
alight as birds

shiny turns
sough of spirits
bright leaves
ready to liberate
the cucumbers
on the fence
cabbage and potatoes
in the garden
pillagers of liberty
tormented by falsity
mocked the chronic
catholic bay
of metes and bounds
over native land

soldiers shiver
rain soaked
down to the waist
wooly and pungent
return from patrol
weary and insecure
major wilkinson
ordered the regiment
to stack weapons
by regimental count
and build fires
unarmed for lunch
steamy bodies
heavy smoke
spread across

the garden
when a single shot
cracked near the cabin
started by chance
the last war
between natives
and the united states

the new york times
reported hearsay
about the indian war
at sugar point
capital news
imagined scenes
at a great distance
headlines raved
troops battle savages
rumored massacre
of one hundred men
and boldly inquired
in banner type
is general bacon dead

bacon survived
the texas indian wars
and the one day
war at sugar point
with only a bullet
crease on his hat
but major wilkinson

fully exposed
by chancy duty
wounded three times
and five soldiers
died in the garden
cold and hungry
outsmarted by birds
hole in the day
and by my heart
above the war
in the bright leaves

william hascal brill
associated press
reported one recruit
failed to engage
a safety catch
on a krag jorgensen
a new norwegian
magazine rifle
issued to the infantry
a few years earlier
in time for cuba
knights of imperialism
tropical adventurers
rough riders
by cinch and errantry

the stack of three
rifles gave way

and one discharged
fortuitously
on the ground
the pillagers
bear island warriors
winchesters ready
at the tree line
returned the fire
brill reported
the major shouted
my god they're fighting
get behind a stump
quick or you will be killed
wilkinson cast aside
his regulation sword
on the sandy point
and rushed headlong
to his death
in the garden war
at sugar point

private wicker
described the start
of subsidiary war
cartridges removed
stacked arms
a nervous recruit
failed to draw
the chamber round
one shot fired

by chance
ominous silence
then a volley
into our ranks
we were surrounded
by the enemy

general bacon
mustered the soldiers
krag in hand
shouted and rallied
under heavy fire
steady boys steady
don't waste
your ammunition
by my heart
an elusive raven
and nineteen natives
circled the garden
hidden in the brush
and waited
behind the maples
a natural camouflage
traces of smoke
floated in the leaves
precise crack
of native winchesters

hole in the day
and pillager warriors

told another story
the war started
when soldiers fired
at native women
unarmed in a canoe
close to the flora
moored at bear island
near the narrows
steadfast pleas
to release a prisoner
by native songs
a captured relative
makwa the bear

lieutenant ross
commander
of the left flank
over the turnips
major wilkinson
center of the war
over cabbages
nurtured that season
by hole in the day
colonel sheehan
right flank
over the potatoes
exposed to fire
summoned
immigrant recruits
by their bravery

and frontline strategy
to scorn and dare
the ghostly enemy
gusts and hidden reign
of winchesters
nothing more
that cold october
but the fear of death
in a native garden

william butler
delivered a message
to lieutenant ross
on the left flank
exposed in turnips
sergeant butler
shot dead in the head
the first casualty
in a war of conceit
the warrior
who fired the shot
raised his arms
at the tree line
shouted and waved
at the blue soldiers
and feigned
his own death
an ironic war game
blaze of maples

oscar burkhard
the hospital steward
towed bodies
and the wounded
across the garden
over cabbages
foot by bloody foot
to the cabin
for medical care
and much later
the immigrant private
was awarded an ironic
medal of honor
bravery in action
against hostile indians

major wilkinson
about the same age
as hole in the day
bravely tread
by martial counts
over cabbage
hearten the soldiers
by swagger and shouts
give it to them boys
give 'em hell
we've got 'em licked
give 'em hell
wilkinson was shot
in the right arm

a flesh wound
minutes later
a second bullet
struck his left thigh
above the knee
two wounds dressed
the lame major
limped back
on the garden line
and was shot
a third time
the winchester slug
burst his belly
a mortal wound
give 'em hell
he shouted twice
to general bacon
his last breath of war
a military salute

boy river warrior
wore an oversized
white shirt
and stood alone
on a fence rail
over the cucumbers
boldly at the back
of the garden
taunted the soldiers
shouted in anishinaabe

mocked and laughed
at the soldiers
gichi mookomaan
white american
as bullets cut
and scorched
the cold air
around his body
the boy river turned
slowly to the leaves
untouched by fury
and walked away
into the thick brush

colonel tinker
craven federal agents
and bystanders
escaped native fire
near bear island
and steamed safely
back to walker
on the flora
deserted the war
and wounded soldiers
overnight on sugar point
with no provisions

general bacon
ordered the soldiers
to dig trenches

among the potatoes
and bruised cabbages
cold and silent
an indian policeman
trustworthy christian
to federal agents
mistakenly shot dead
by an immigrant sentry
face of the enemy
a native in the dark
on treaty land
the only native casualty
in the war
blindly forsaken
by soldiers
and timber grafters
near the midewigaan
of hole in the day

nineteen natives
bear island pillagers
defeated eighty
third infantry
officers and soldiers
blue immigrants
mean citizens
newspaper reporters
cornered that autumn
in a bloody garden
hole in the day

by my heart
trace of native shamans
soared overhead
with the ravens
in the white pine
and mighty maples

Gatling Gun

6 OCTOBER 1898

lieutenant colonel
abram horbach
returned a salute
boarded a slow train
for walker
and leech lake
endowed by fidelity
dominion duty
two hundred
soldiers of destiny
clumsy and rustic
with empire weapons
and a gatling gun
arrived in time
to honor the dead
and badly wounded
mostly immigrants
never to fight
hole in the day
bear island pillagers
the chance war
closed overnight
third infantry
cold and bloody
routed by natives
at sugar point

sentries posted
trenches cut
across the garden
scent of cabbage
bloody blue wool
dusted with snow
silent counts
by wounded soldiers
newspaper storiers
side by side
overnight
in a dark cabin
haunted by natives
sound of sacred rattles
zhiishiigwan
a medicine dance
hole in the day
by my heart
in the white pine

daniel schallenstocker
german born
foolhardy private
the last casualty
after four months
in uniform
that early morning
cold and snowy
cornered and crazed
regiment in ruins

shied in a cabin
by hideaway words
beside the dead
and ghastly moans
of the wounded
daniel broke ranks
at first light
driven by hunger
harvest game
reached out to secure
a tiny bounty
of frosty potatoes
and survived
a native mercy shot
creased the earth
near his dirty hand
emboldened by chance
and godly reason
he crouched lower
reached again
to pluck a meal
the second bullet
struck his back
heart burst
blood spurted
on his hands
blue and steamy
catch of shame
choked once
on a faint word

maybe a name
and died alone
in a native garden
forever hungry
at twenty nine

the native warrior
who fired the shot
was only fifteen
the pillager son
of hole in the day
he waited
with his winchester
at the tree line
in the dark maples
for a wild soldier
and fired once
to forewarn
the military poachers
the second round
was the last and deadly
shot of the war
that cold morning
at sugar point

the flora listed
bounced and roared
against the dock
once more
at walker bay

sixteen casualties
treated on deck
behind the ramparts
hay bales
one brevet officer
five soldiers
dead and covered
bloody blue
crusade of shame
a chance war
provoked by arrogance
federal agents
greedy grafters
mercenaries
of the white pine

chief white cloud
waubanaquot
anishinaabe ogimaa
white earth reservation
a native patriot
of natural reason
died at the agency
on his way
to mediate peace
with the army
pillager warriors
and federal agents

chief white cloud
great storier of peace
native heir of the third
white fisher
and descendant
of the second
hole in the day
touched by visions
midewiwin ceremonies
spirit healers
teased the seasons
and catholics
by tricky stories
morning coats
survivance treaties
and soared
with the cranes
at sunrise
over sugar point
everlasting memories
of that war
a continental shimmer
of native liberty

War Necklace

9 OCTOBER 1898

hole in the day
undaunted warrior
pillager of liberty
returned at sunrise
with the ravens
to his garden
cabbage cut
potatoes plundered
midewigaan
cabin bloodied
by soldiers
traces of dead
blue savages
at sugar point

medicine bundles
midewayaan
miigis and otter
eagle feathers
stolen and stained
sacred stories
trickster creations
corrupted
by nervy soldiers
routed at last
by pillager bears

hole in the day
gathered cucumbers
and spent shells
from newly issued
krag jorgensens
cast among
bloody potatoes
and wounded cabbages
fashioned a memorial
war necklace
native survivance
remembrance
a defeated army
overcome by winchesters
and fierce irony

private wicker
wrote that natives
rightly fought
for their land
and mighty trees
an errant sentiment
shared by many
blue soldiers
after the war
at sugar point
the rightful owners
of this country
were mistreated
defrauded and robbed

natives turned
their wrath against
united states soldiers

private wicker
confessed the dread
to fire my gun
at the unfortunate
red man
he was fighting
for the land
the rights
were his
fighting it is true
in his own peculiar
and treacherous way

private wicker
stole eagle feathers
sacred miigwan
accursed booty
from the dark
ceremonial cabin
midewigaan
of hole in the day

private oscar burkhard
immigrant soldier
born in germany
stole sacred drums

mitigwakik
from the cabin
perverse medical booty
at the time
and was awarded
a medal of honor
for his bravery

doctor herbert harris
regimental surgeon
stole a sacred
birch bark scroll
songs of the anishinaabe
midewiwin ceremonies
the absolute savagery
of a combat healer

one soldier
easily recovered
from his wounds
nine others
shot in the neck
shoulder
face and thigh
ankle and leg
survived their wounds
but were forever
crippled
mind and body
by military conceit

sergeant leroy ayers
flesh wound
on his left leg
the only combat
regiment veteran
who served
in the santiago de cuba
military campaign

herman antonelli
immigrant private
born in italy
shot in the leg
at thirty four

private edward brown
born in chicago
shot in the lower face
cut his tongue
shattered his teeth
at twenty one

private john daly
born in wisconsin
shot in the thigh
shattered the bone
disabled at twenty two

private jens jensen
enlisted in minneapolis

a daredevil recruit
shot in the shoulder
at twenty two

private charles turner
born in wisconsin
shot in the shoulder
shattered bones
disabled at twenty four

private george wicker
born in wisconsin
flesh wound
on the left ankle
at twenty one

private richard boucher
born in canada
shot in the neck
nasty wound
torn flesh
slow to heal
at twenty six

the most reverend
pleasant hunter
westminster presbyterian
chapel in minneapolis
conducted services
for the dead soldiers

the third infantry band
obediently played
a funeral march
weary field officers
mounted on horseback
led the cortege
honor guards
escorted the bodies
and fired a last salute
over the graves
at fort snelling

sergeant william butler
born in michigan
died thirty two years later
at sugar point
a model soldier
served three years
in the first cavalry
at fort custer
and then enlisted
in the third infantry

private john onsted
born in norway
shot dead in the neck
severed veins
bloody blue uniform
relatives notified

daniel schallenstocker
born in germany
enlisted four months
before the war
dead at twenty nine
no relatives

private albert ziebel
born in germany
enlisted three months
before a bullet
severed an artery
in his left leg
bloody footprints
in the garden
dead at twenty seven

private edward lowe
born a farmer
served three years
favorite soldier
shot in the neck
dead at thirty two
relatives await
his return to illinois

brevet major
melville wilkinson
born in new york
civil war veteran

promoted for gallantry
against natives
died at sugar point
buried in separate
military ceremonies

many immigrants
farmers and adventurers
turned soldier
dead and wounded
in a treacherous
emissary war
over the chance
discharge of a rifle
wicked agents
timber barons
cruel renunciation
of native reason
treaty rights
and continental liberty
forever haunted
by discovery
cultural conceit
and constitutional trickery

Gerald Vizenor is professor emeritus at the University of California, Berkeley, and professor of American Studies at the University of New Mexico. He is the author of *Bearheart* (1990), *Griever* (1990), *Interior Landscapes* (1990), and *The People Named the Chippewa* (1984), all published by the University of Minnesota Press.

❖

Jace Weaver is professor of Native American cultures at the University of Georgia.